I SAW A PORN THAT STARTED THAT WAY

RIDICULOUS STORIES OF A REAL-LIFE CABLE GUY

E.C. DOUGLAS

CHANNEL GUIDE/FORWARD

Firstly, let me start off by saying that this book is 100% a work of truth. Well, the truth as I remember it. Let me be a bit more serious for a minute. These are stories as I remember them - names and places have been changed to protect the guilty. I may or may not embellish here or there to make the story a little more exciting or funny at times or for better flow but my promise to you is that the kernel of the story and the most pertinent details will remain unchanged.

All of this happened on real jobs, real calls that I was sent on and worked on over my years as a cable tv, internet and home phone installer/repair technician.

The title of this book started as a kind of joke

amongst my friends and me. It goes something like this:

"Did you see the porno where the Cable guy shows up at the super model's house?"

"No."

"Well, he knocks on the door and she answers it wearing barely any clothes, just a hint of a robe with some exotic scent wafting from her body. She says 'thank god you're here to service me'. Then he goes inside and fixes the cable."

Ha ha ha. Big laugh. But it really got me thinking. There are a lot of crazy stories and experiences that I've had over my 18+ year career as a telecom technician—I really should write them down! People are always curious about the weirdos, perverts, hoarders, etc.

Anytime I tell one of these stories at a party— usually people don't believe me, or they laugh hysterically, or some other reaction, but the stories always get a strong reaction.

I figured that level of feedback must mean I'm onto something interesting. Getting a "peek behind the curtain", such that it is, of a dying breed of in-home service personnel must interest at least a few people...more-so when the story involves some salacious detail, disgusting hoarded mess, or weird behaviour.

At a bare minimum I've had a good time putting these stories to paper (or ones and zeroes at the very least) and hopefully long after I'm gone they will serve as a testament to some of the crazy stuff that I and my brothers and sisters had to deal with on a daily basis.

This book is not necessarily meant to be read front to back in a traditional "novel" manner. You can read this book front to back if you wish; but there is no specific through-line. Each story will stand on its own and so this book is meant to be read in bite-sized chunks. Story by story, as you see fit.

Well—that's enough preamble, let's get to it!

Oh last thing real quick: thanks for purchasing my book! I'm really excited to share these stories with you!

Yours,

E.C. Douglas

CONTENTS

THE COLLECTOR

It was a cold and grey February day. I had been assigned a trouble call at a city-owned low-income rental complex just off of downtown in an "ok" area of town. It was midday and I had just finished my lunch, so I was fuelled up and ready to tackle a few more jobs before the end of my shift. This particular complex is typical of public-owned facilities—just institutional enough so you know that it's publicly-owned yet just friendly enough so you don't feel like you are entering a penitentiary. So the grounds and complex were generally in decent if not somewhat dilapidated shape, especially since the facility had been built in the late sixties to early seventies. You know the kind of institutional grey or light brown brick buildings I'm talking about? They all have the same basic tidy landscaping that is kept neat and trimmed but with slightly oversized seating made of concrete and plastic. Not that you could see the landscaping or sit outside since there was about 2 feet of snow outside and it was currently about 20 points below freezing. However the sidewalks had been neatly shovelled and salted so it was an easy walk from my van to the entrance.

I expected that this call would be an easy one, as the TV decoder box I was there to service was just showing as "non-functional" in our testing system, but I could see that everything else in the home was working. Since I knew the building and the particulars of the economic situation of most of its residents I knew that I could be in for a bit of a messy, unkempt unit. (Not all the tenants of these facilities are messy or gross of course, but I find many are.) I had my hopes that this call wouldn't be too gross and that it would in fact, be an "in-and-out" call.

There were 6 units on the outside of the building to either side of the front entrance on the ground floor with parking stalls just in front, set up almost like a motel. As I walked to the main entrance, I suspected that the unit I would be servicing was on the outside ring of the building, rather than in the main tower. I never enjoy working in these units, because in the summer your fry, and in the winter you bake. Since these units are on the outside of the building surrounding the inner courtyard, there is limited insulation to protect them from the elements. Usually, that means the tenants have to crank up the heat in the winter to keep the place warm, which I don't blame them for, but it usually means that the unit is 10–15 degrees warmer than room temperature, and there is no way to work inside without taking off all of your outside gear…even on an "in-and-out".

So I buzzed the unit and the fellow confirmed that he was on the outside ring, and that he'd open his door so I could find him. I started walking toward his unit and I could see a hand sticking out from the wall approximately where I figured the unit should be. My first inkling that all was not right happened when I was about 20 or so feet from the door. I could smell the heavy, acrid, thick nicotine from decades of smoking. I hoped it was emanating from another unit. The second thing, and I didn't think much of it at the time, was a very brief waft of the sharp smell of urine. Being as cold as it was outside, it passed quickly, and I wrote it off as a cat or other animal having peed on one of the large concrete and plastic outside seating fixtures I was passing on my left.

However, as I came up to the door on my right and turned my body to face the gentleman in the doorway, the full-on, angry scent of urine and decades-old stale smoke forced by the rush of hot air coming from inside the apartment, hit me full in the face like the hardened fist of a prize fighter. I reeled back a few steps before catching myself and extending my business card to introduce myself. The fella said his name, but I didn't hear him as it was all I could do to stand straight and not fall over, struggling to keep my eyes open against the burn of the airborne urine. I had no idea that anything could be that pungent. He invited me inside and told me not to worry about my shoes as his cleaning lady would be in later that day. (As if a cleaning lady had ever touched this place???) While not the most disgusting apartment I had ever been in, it was close. Old pizza boxes strewn about, leftover food on plates, clothes hanging off everything, and garbage bags open and full of trash everywhere. I wouldn't call it a "hoarder home", but it was getting there.

Already sweating form the excessive heat, I asked to see the box that was causing the issue. Luckily for me it was only a 2 room apartment unit, so it was small enough that I could likely get in and out quickly. There was a kitchenette/dining area and a living room/bedroom area, with a small water closet off the main entrance hall. I should mention at this point that the smell of urine was getting stronger. I asked if he had a cat, and he said no, which I thought was strange.

As I entered the living room/bedroom I saw them. Dozens of plastic half-gallon hospital supply urine collection bottles—uncapped, lined up along all the walls of his apartment, sitting on the floor, and FULL of urine. FULL. OF. URINE. It was all I could do to hold back a gag and keep a straight face. Thankfully, he had his TV on, but clearly the cable box was not working. So I unplugged it quickly and told him he'd need a new box as I grabbed it and ran from the unit, about to vomit. I made it all the way to my van before I spewed my lunch everywhere. I couldn't help it—the smell of stale cigarette smoke and that much urine mixed together in that sweltering heat pushed me over the top. I now know why they ask you NEVER to pee in a sauna!!!!

As I gathered my wits, I made a plan to hold my breath, get into the unit, plug the box in, and make an excuse as to why I needed to go back to my van again while the box booted up. I grabbed the replacement box and slowly shambled with grim determination, like a prisoner marching the green mile, back toward the unit. I hyperventilated myself just outside the apartment, took a huge deep breath and held it in. Hoping I could hold it long enough, I took the plunge back into the piss-sauna. I ran inside, plugged in the box, told the customer I needed to go back to my computer in the van while the box booted itself up, and that I would be a few minutes while I ran some diagnostics, then bee lined it for the door. I made it to the van, this time without puking.

I waited probably 10 minutes to be sure the box had time to boot up. Lucky for me, it did and I could query it from the backend system. I ran my tests from the laptop in the van— everything passed—I was nearly home free! All that remained was to go back and do the wrap-up with the customer. I opened his front door and shouted to him. I thanked him for his patience, apologized for the inconvenience, told him the job was complete, and then turned and booked it to my van as fast as my feet would allow!

2
_____

THE RELIC

Older ladies are so sweet. More often than not they will offer me cookies and milk as I work, or try to slip a twenty dollar bill into my back pocket as a tip. (Although I suspect that the widows are usually just trying to cop a feel.)

This particular installation was for a stereotypical blue-haired grandmother. I was switching services over for her from our competitors. The entire install went without incident—everything was complete and I was wrapping up my education portion—where I explain how to use our services and make sure the customer is familiar with our remote and the big one: how to order pay-per-view!

All was well. I was especially pleased that Mildred seemed to grasp the concept of our TV system much better than many folks half her age. As

I was closing my usual spiel she interrupted me and asked if I could help get her computer online. "Of course! I would be happy to!", I answered sheepishly. You see, I had failed to ask if she had any wifi devices that needed to be reconnected to our new wifi router, so I felt kinda silly.

Mildred led me to her office explaining that she didn't do much "on the line," explaining that her husband used to deal with all of the bills and the emailing and so forth. She continued to explain that he had recently passed away and this was the first "technical" thing she had to do since his passing. I said I understood, of course, and would be happy to show her the basics of internet usage as well. As she opened the door to the office I was very surprised to see an old Commodore 64 sitting on her desk, humming and buzzing as if it were 1982—green CRT display and all! At this point Mildred asked if this computer would be sufficient to get the emails from her grandkids. I was dumbstruck and I literally had no words. I was searching my company approved explanations and metaphors databank in my brain, trying to come up with an explanation about why this computer wouldn't work for modern usage…

Well—Mildred must have seen the look of sheer terror in my eyes because she started to crack up. She laughed so hard that tears started streaming down her face as she pulled a brand new shiny iPhone out of her back pocket.

So Mildred says to me: "I know that computer is too old to do anything, my husband used to like to use it for something or other, that's why we kept it all these years. I just wanted to play a little joke on you; my real internet connectivity is on my iPhone and iPad. Oh, you should see the look on your face! Imagine! An old Commodore 64 getting on the internet! Ha Ha Ha."

Lulz Mildred. Points to you for getting me with that one.

Some older folks still have a VERY mischievous sense of humour. To be honest, she really did get me on that one though. The setup was perfect and we both had a good laugh once the cat was out of the bag.

I gave her the WiFi information that she needed and all was good.

As I turned to leave a felt a little pinch on my behind and sure enough there was a folded up twenty dollar bill in my back pocket. As I turned around she winked at me and said: "Go get yourself a coffee, you worked hard today", and that is exactly what I did.

3

THE NUDISTS

This will be a short story. Unlike many of the other stories in this collection, I just want to get to the point; honestly it's shocking enough without any other description or lead up. Let me also preface this by saying—I in no way judge people by what they choose to do in the privacy of their own homes, nor do I judge what people do in public, so long as it doesn't hurt me or others, frankly I don't give a damn!

So I was sent to a call in an average suburban neighbourhood, to an average suburban home. In fact, the house probably looks a lot like yours, with a small front porch and a door like any other. When I walked up the steps and knocked on the door, I heard a few footsteps and a little rustling inside, then the door opened and a man stood there—completely nude.

I apologized and told him I'd give him a couple of minutes to prepare, and I'd come back after he's had a chance to get ready.

He looked at me, with a straight face, no hint of sarcasm or malice says "oh, don't worry, we're nudists this is completely normal."

Again, as I mentioned—I don't judge people for what they do in their own homes and if he was ok with it, then I was ok with it; after all I'm wasn't there to hang out with him—I was there to work on his TV and internet services.

After I'd been in the home for a few minutes and working on the TV in the living room, I noticed there was a woman's voice also in the home. I wondered to myself if she'd be naked too. Well, I didn't have to wonder too long, as she walked into their living room in all her bare-naked glory and offered me a drink from a silver tray. I thanked her, had a sip, and set the glass back down on the tray, as I noticed three children run by the living room also completely naked! These weren't young adults or teenagers, likely only 3-5 years old, and I expected they didn't know any different so it was normal for them to be running around naked, playing tag or whatever they were doing.

As I finished up my repair (I couldn't have been there for much more than an hour) the entire family came to the front door to thank me for my work and see me off.

I'm pretty sure that as I left I heard one of the children say to his mum something to the effect of: "that man was very weird, he wore his clothes the whole time he was here." The mom shushed him and told him that because I was working for a company and as I was on a service call, I was required to wear my clothes and safety shoes, but if I had had a choice I too likely would have been naked.

4

THE MONSTER UNDER THE BED

Do you ever have one of those days where nothing is going right, where you spill your coffee, your car won't start, you break your glasses, and you forget something super important at home that you needed for your big presentation that morning? Well, I was having one of those days—nothing was going right. I made my coffee that morning but forgot it on my counter, and didn't realize until I'd driven away from home and was already 15 minutes into the drive to my first customer's home. I couldn't get things repaired for one reason or another, orders were screwed up, and I couldn't get services up and working for new customers. It was just an absolute gong-show of a day. So I decided that I needed a reset. I stopped and had lunch at a cafe, relaxed for a few minutes, and enjoyed some good food and a much needed coffee (finally!) I promised myself that no matter what happened, my next job would go smoothly, and even if it didn't, I would face it with a smile and not let it get me down.

I arrived at the older low-rise apartment complex a few minutes early for my appointment and called the woman whose services I was there to repair; we'll call her Sarah. She answered the phone on the last possible ring, slightly out of breath as though she had just been jogging lightly, or perhaps doing aerobics in the living room. I didn't pay much attention, but told her I was on site and would be on my way up to the apartment in a few moments. Gathering my tools, I entered the building and made my way up the 4 flights of stairs to the top floor. No wonder Sarah had been out of breath—she likely had just got home herself and was running up those 4 flights to catch the ringing phone, likely scared that she'd miss me. Trust me when I say that the days of the telephone or cable repair man showing up, knocking on the door once and then leaving are over! It takes more paperwork and phone calls to incomplete a job because the customer is not home, than to just stick around for 10, 15 or even 30 minutes and wait for a customer. But that's not part of our story here.

Sarah was a typical early-to-mid-forties single

woman done up in the contemporary style like "housewives of some city"—hair, makeup, nails, possibly some light cosmetic enhancement, or just good genes and no kids. She lived alone with a couple of cats in a nicely decorated, albeit small apartment. She was dressed not in professional or office clothing but in very snuggly fitted Playboy™ branded lounge wear that seemed to have to stretch just a little more around her gifted or enhanced curves. I only mention this because I thought it odd for her to be wearing this type of clothing if she had just been at work, and she didn't strike me as a "dancer". Later I would find out she worked in the travel industry as a travel agent. I noticed theheavy scent of perfume and musk when I entered the unit. It wasn't unpleasant, and the place didn't smell like cat urine, so I was very pleased indeed!

I was on the job to repair a TV box that wasn't functioning in her bedroom, and I could see almost immediately it was because one of her cats had chewed through the cable line running from the living room to the bedroom. The entire time we were talking I got the sensation that Sarah was trying to seduce me, or at least feel me out or flirt with me for fun. She would say things like "I'm so glad you're here to service me" or "you look like such a strong young man, I'm sure you could teach me a thing or two…about my cable" with a wink. I'm not a bad looking guy and I'm usually in pretty decent shape, but this type of thing only happens in porno movies so it wasn't really something I even acknowledged at the time. It wasn't until later that I would reflect on it and realize what she might have been trying to do, or perhaps what she successfully did. (More on that in a bit.)

So I tell her that I have to enter the bedroom to get at the cable to fix the service line, and she agrees to let me in there saying "you can do anything you want in my bedroom, feel free to just throw things around," and then she disappears around the corner into the main living room area. It's about the time that I'm tracing the path of the cable around the edge of the room to the bed where it disappears underneath, that a cat screeches out from under the bed with a pair of g-string, thong-type panties caught around it's neck. I smile and giggle a little to myself, even though she didn't see that I saw. But then as I'm bending down to get at the cable outlet I hear a slight whimpering moan coming from the living room area of the apartment. I decided to ignore it, because I can also hear a slightly wet and rhythmic squishing sound coming from the same room. I assume that it's just my imagination and I decide it's not worth it to check out because at this point I just want to fix this lady's cable and get out of this apartment. The last thing I need to do is walk in on her pleasuring herself! Why someone would do this with a stranger in their home is beyond me. But I'm fairly positive that was exactly what was going on.

So back to the outlet under the bed—as I pull back the little bed skirt I notice a clear plastic tote under the bed with what must have been about 100 sex toys in it! And low and behold, right there between me and the cable outlet, is the largest silicon phallus I have ever seen! Easily 10 times the size of a real male member, lying on it's side and sparkling in the light of my flashlight. I had no choice but to move it to the side so I could get to the cable jack. As I reached out to it, I noticed that it was slick with what I assume was lubricant, or possibly bodily fluid and it must have weighed at least 10 pounds! I immediately grabbed some hand sanitizer from my tool box and cleaned my hand. At least it wasn't shit!

I finished up with the repair, and exited the room to go back to the main living area and hallway of the apartment. Sarah was now laid back on the couch, smoking a cigarette with the window open. The smell of musk was now even stronger and only slightly covered up by the cigarette smoke, but a window was open so the fresh air was streaming in rapidly to freshen up the room. She looked at me, asking if I had seen everything I needed to in her bedroom. I replied that I had. As I explained the repair and was handing her my business card before leaving, I noticed a bright orange silicon penis replica (this one more normal sized, still on the large end of the spectrum, but with comically large testes) on the coffee table, standing erect on it's suction cup base. I made no mention of it and neither did she, although she did thank me for my time and asked if I'd like to come back later for a little "get together" she was having with just a few male co-workers and herself. I politely declined—but I was pretty sure she had just invited me to take part in a gang bang.

Suffice it to say, although it was a little weird, it definitely brightened my mood and made me laugh hysterically when I got back to my truck. The rest of my day went perfectly smoothly !

ADDENDUM: About 3 years later, after I had forgotten about this entire incident I went to an agency to book a vacation for my wife and I. Wouldn't you know it - Sarah was the agent that booked our flights and hotels! I don't think she remembered me (since I wasn't in my company uniform and my facial hair situation had changed dramatically!) But I sure remembered her! HA!

THE BASEMENT

I could write chapters upon chapters about my experience with people and their shitty little fur "babies". Most people are very respectful of your space and will ask nicely, "are you ok with dogs?" Inevitably though, especially if you are there for a long time, they eventually let the little hell raisers out. OR they give you just a pubic hair length of time after you finish saying "it should be ok" before they unleash their hell hound to run full bore at you, nose first, like a fur rocket right into your crotch. Or to jump all over you and attempt to lick you to death.

Or like the time when after I had my vasectomy and I had to return to work before I was fully healed because my manager "couldn't have any more sick days on his roster that close to the end of the quarter", and the couple I was doing a repair for let their GIANT Great Dane jump at me and land a huge paw right on my junk, ripping a stitch and causing a very alarming amount of bleeding. (At least I got 1 personal day off and a weekend to sort-of recover!! I guess that will teach me to have minor medical procedures!!!)

Anyway—back to the story—this happened toward the end of winter when the air during the day is in positive temperatures but there is still snow on the ground, and the evenings and nights are still below zero.

This home was an unremarkable, rather small 2 story build on a large lot, in what used to be, 30-ish years ago, the suburbs, but was now almost "inner city" by most accounts. I noticed the deck railings, the doorway, the stairs, and nearly every surface from about 2-3 feet down had been chewed/gnawed on by what I can only assume were dogs (I never saw them as these people were kind enough to lock them outside in the back yard for my entire visit—a VERY rare occurrence let me tell you!) The house was not especially dirty but there was a distinct *funk* emanating from every room; I could not put my finger on it, but it lay somewhere between rotting food and old, wet grass. Strange, but I went about my repair work unfazed because I am now immune to the smells in most people's homes.

Now, for many repairs, especially for folks with dogs/cats, the repairs are very obvious as their "little buddy" has chewed through a line in the room with the box; but in other cases I need to get outside and trace lines, or go into the basement to find a splitter or a filter that might have failed or was never installed in the first place. Sadly, this was one of those times that I needed to get into the basement. The homeowners were reluctant to grant me access to the basement, but eventually acquiesced when I told them if I couldn't get into the basement, I couldn't fix their cable.

The husband tells me he'll go first and opens the door, turning on the light and walking down ahead of me. I notice that as he goes down he grabs a big snow shovel from the wall, and as we get further down the flight of stairs I notice the smell is getting stronger and that's when I finally see the cause of the funk in this premises. Instead of letting their dogs out to the backyard at night (presumably because it was too cold) they simply let the dogs down into the basement to use the ENTIRE unfinished basement like a giant "litter box", except without any sand/gravel and just piles of shit all over the floor. Only, this hadn't been going on for just this past winter, *no way*, this had been going on for **years,** and I suspect that it wasn't just during the winter. I think it was whenever these two lazy fuckers didn't feel like going outside (which I presume was OFTEN) because their entire basement floor was covered in inches of shit, and in a few corners and other areas there were patches of mushrooms growing in it/on it!

So that's what the snow shovel is for??? I must have said it out loud because the husband kind of nervously laughed and said "yeah..." then asked where I needed to go and started shovelling me a path toward the main electrical panel, as this was where I assumed I needed to work (thankfully I was right). It was like he was shovelling me a path through freshly fallen snow, except that he wasn't! HA! I replaced the filter, and got the hell out of there as fast as I could politely excuse myself. These people did NOT get a card for followup with me. I did hear through the grapevine that another co-worker of mine had returned to this very house several years after I was there and confirmed that the shit carpet was still fully covering their basement floor - but now had worked its way up into the main part of the house as well!

I will never understand some people.

THE TIPPER

It is not company policy to allow us to accept tips. However, in some circumstances it's considered very rude culturally to not accept a gratuity, whether it be a drink, a snack, or a small some of money, and if it's less than a certain amount we are allowed to accept, after refusing at least 2 times.

On this particular day—I was helping an elderly lady with programming her remote (in actual fact I was just showing her how to change channels for the 3rd or 4th time—can't remember now how many techs had been there before me. However, as I finished and was leaving, she insisted on giving me a tip. I of course politely refused twice, and then on the third time accepted and said thank you.

This was a strange tip in that it was like a miniature business-size document envelope, perhaps 6X8, (most people just thrust some greasy cash into your palm, or give you a cola or something) and it had a lump in the bottom. I waited until I got out to my van to look inside. Inside was a "watchtower" magazine (the Jehovah Witness cult propaganda magazine), a hand crocheted cross, and an old, stale, 3 years past it's expiry date granola bar! HA!

Suffice it to say - the entire package was thrown directly out into the trash at my next stop to the warehouse. I now only accept cash in bills! HA HA!

RACIST SHIT PEOPLE SAY

People are racist. I'm racist, you're racist, she's racist, he's racist. If you're thinking "he's an idiot, I'm not a racist" - you are MOST DEFI-NITELY A RACIST! We're all racist against others that are not "like" us, from other countries, people that have a different culture—hell we're even racist against our "own kind" that come from the "wrong part of town". It's one of our great strengths as a species, the ability to pick out patterns and find like-ness to keep our tribes together. But it's also an old, outdated, outmoded and no longer needed form of classification in this day and age. It hasn't been needed for perhaps hundreds of years - yet we continue to use it for political agendas, news head-lines and other bullshit. This is a collection of some of the funnier racist shit I've heard from customers over the years. Sad to report, I hear something like this every. Damn. Day.

Brown Customer: "I'm so glad you're here."

Me: "Of course, I'm going to work hard to fix your issue."

Brown Customer: "No I mean, you, a white guy, those brown guys that show up are lazy and always do a shitty job."

Old White Guy: "I'm so glad you're here. I'm not racist, but I can't talk to those other techs. It's nice to have a white man here that I can talk to." I should mention he had one of the thickest European accents I'd ever heard—he clearly was foreign born.

Old Chinese Lady: "Oh good, you're not black!"

Old Black Lady: "Oh good, you're not Chinese."

Old Brown Lady: "Oh, you're white—I wanted a brown tech so I can talk to him in my own language."

. . .

OLD CHINESE MAN: "该死的！ 我想要一个能说普通话的技术人员！"

OLD JAPANESE MAN: "あなたはおそらく日本語が理解できないでしょう私は日本語を話す技術者を頼みました！(YOU PROBABLY CAN'T UNDERSTAND JAPANESE, I ASKED FOR A JAPANESE TECHNICIAN!)

Me: "大丈夫です - 私は日本語がわかります!" (IT'S OK. I UNDERSTAND JAPANESE!)

Old Japanese Man: "日本語がわからない!" (YOU CAN'T UNDERSTAND JAPANESE!)

Me: "私はあなたが私が理解できることを保証します！"(NO, I REALLY CAN UNDERSTAND!)

Old Japanese Man: "くそー、私は再予約して、もう一度日本人に依頼しなければならないでしょう。"(DAMN IT, I WILL HAVE TO RESCHEDULE AND ASK FOR A JAPANESE PERSON AGAIN.)

Me: "… Ok then I guess I will go ahead and cancel your appointment! "

Old Japanese Man: " Ok."

OLD WHITE LADY: "It's so nice to have you here to fix my service instead of one of them."

Me: "…uh…"

OLD WHITE LADY: "You know the last black tech I had in my home stole from me."

OLD BLACK LADY: "Get out of my house, cracker!"

OLD WHITE GUY: "It's so nice that you have a regular name instead of something I can't pronounce. I'm not racist, but it's just nice to be able to understand your name."

8

THE LISTENERS

*S*ometimes you get a call that leaves you scratching your head. Not because you couldn't figure out the issue, or get an install completed, but because the customer was so odd that you just couldn't figure out if it was for real or if it was a gag! This is one of those stories.

I was sent on a repair ticket for internet services to a large home in one of the nicer, more affluent neighbourhoods of the city, with ticket notes of "chronic repeat, customer extremely agitated, says someone has hacked their internet. Customer demanding tech."

I always hate these calls because you know you're going to be dealing with an irate customer who hasn't had the resolution they want (even it if isn't a resolution we can actually provide) who wants to make your life hell, and to call in and leave you a bad review once you've left, and then will call in for another tech visit after you've gone giving your metrics a ding because you've had a "repeat call". Anyway I wasn't sure there was anything I could do —after all I work for the ISP, that's internet service *provider*, not the internet/software police. We merely provide service to the home—it's up to the customer to decide how they want to connect to the web (computer, smart phone, tablet, smart tv, etc. etc. etc) So software bug/glitch calls usually are a pretty quick verification/diagnostic visit of about 30 minutes to make sure all of the contracted services are working, and then a bill to the customer for my time, since there is nothing wrong with the service as promised. (Provided I don't find any issues)

So, I arrive at the home and stroll up to the front door with my business card and laptop in hand, ready to verify their services. I ring the doorbell and wait. And wait. And wait. And wait.

After about 15 minutes and 3 or 4 more rings of the doorbell, knocks on the door, and calls to a cellphone that wasn't turned on, I was about to leave when suddenly the door jerked open and a woman wearing a large, hooded robe, dark sunglasses and a scarf, as well as gloves, looks at me, looks up at the sky, grabs me by the shirt collar and yanks me into the entranceway as she proclaims "get in here before they see me."

Oh. Shit.

So Trudy (we'll call her Trudy) explains that you can never be too careful because "they are always watching her," and she apologized that she kept me waiting, but she had to be sure I was really from the IPT before she could let me in. (Don't know what she meant by that, as it is not a term used by my company for *anything*.) So Trudy explains that her home has been hacked, and that "they" are listening to her from every room and from every appliance—her TV, her fridge, her stove, her computer (which was in pieces on the living room floor). Clearly, I wasn't dealing with someone who lived on the same plane of reality as I do.

I tried to explain how the internet worked, and that someone would have to have brand new "smart" devices hooked up to the internet for a third party to "hack" them in the first place. Trudy had old appliances from the late 70's, maybe early 80's. So no digital circuitry of any type there. As previously stated, her computer was in pieces, so that wasn't going be used anytime soon. Her TV was an old CRT style built into the wall/cabinet unit, like the kind you used to see at your grandparents or great grandparent's house, with a large wooden housing, and the large silver letters RCA running across the bottom. Clearly, she didn't have digital cable, and this TV couldn't be hacked either. BUT to make her happy I told her I would log into the modem and make sure all the security protocols were still active, and ensure the connection to her home was clean and working up to par, and it was. But this still wasn't good enough.

Trudy was still convinced that "they" were listening, and that I needed to fix this issue for her, and she cried out, and literally cried for me to help her. I considered running for the door, or perhaps even telling her that "they" were on to me too and I was being watched so I couldn't help at this time, and then submitting a report and request that no further techs be sent to this house, because this lady was liable to hurt someone or herself while the tech was on site. (At one point she was crying and caterwauling so violently I thought she might collapse!) But I thought I would take a gamble and see if I could appease her before I left.

All cable techs will have what's called a tone generator and a toner, or a toning wand. It's what we plug into one end of a specific wire run to find the other end at the terminus in amongst all the other wires, because it creates a tone, an almost alarm-type oscillating frequency that can be picked up by the wand. The interesting thing is that it makes a few little beep type noises, and will pick up a little static and electrical hum as you move it around in the air, across walls, etc.

So I decided I was going to do a little slight of hand/illusion/pantomime for Trudy to prove to her once and for all that there were no bugs in her house. I made her get very close and I explained in a very hushed, whispered tone that I understood her problem, and I was going to make sure there were no bugs or problems. I showed her the devices I was going to use, and explained that it was a "bug detector", and that as I moved through the rooms of her home if any bugs would be found I would hear an "alarm", and I turned it on, and placed the wand near the generator. I explained that once I placed the main device at her main electrical panel it would generate that alarm tone, and as my detector got near any of the transmitter devices it would go off, then we could find and disable any bugs that might be present. She bought it hook line and sinker. I placed the tone generator on top of her electrical panel and turned it on, then spent the next 25 minutes with Trudy moving from room to room, conducting "sweeps" to find bugs. I don't think I have to tell you we didn't find any. The look of relief on her face, though, showed me my little gamble had paid off. I collected my tools and excused myself from her presence. She thanked me profusely and closed and locked the door quite quickly as I stepped outside the threshold.

I'm not sure whatever happened to Trudy. I'd look in on the account every once in a while, just to see if she had had any other techs out to visit, and she had not. The account, to my knowledge, is still active. Oh, and in case you were wondering—I didn't charge her a diagnostics fee for my time, as she was clearly not well, and didn't know that she was wasting anyone's time. She just knew she was scared and felt helpless, and she looked to my company to send a professional for help. I feel good that I was able to help her, even if I didn't do anything in reality —but I like to think that my little charade was able to help her sleep more soundly after my visit. Occasionally, amongst all the other filth, shit, piss smell, and weird people - you get to help someone, even if it is just lending an empathetic ear, and that makes a huge difference!

THE NEW SET

$\mathcal{I}$ was working in an upscale neighbourhood of the city one fine summer afternoon, and thinking to myself, that I really enjoyed my job—especially, meeting new and interesting people. I was pulling up to a very large, very modern, very expensive looking home, and imagining what kind of people would be inside. Turns out, I didn't have to wait very long.

The lady of the house came out to greet me in the driveway. Tina, we'll call her, was dressed in the latest fashion including a business-suit style cropped, black jacket, and *very* short, black pencil-skirt. Her hair was done up, full make-up, jewelry and black stiletto heels—she looked like she was about to step onto a photography set to model for an upcoming issue of "Hot Rich Housewives Quarterly." She introduced herself, took my card and casually mentioned "what big strong arms you have there", with a wink. I thought it was a bit strange—but not wholly without precedent as good looking women often flirted with me while I was working, as they thought it would help them get free stuff. There were 2 problems with that: 1, I'm not that cheap, and 2, It's no longer like the old days, everything is digital. I can't "flip a switch" and give out free cable—it's all controlled from the office. Of course, I'll never tell anyone that upfront as I enjoy it, (it's flattering!), and it makes for good stories!

I should also mention at this point Tina was alone in this massive house. She told me her husband was away on business, "he's always away on business" she said with a pouty, fake, lip-out baby doll type of voice. There were no children, no pets, just Tina, alone in this massive house. I politely made some small-talk while Tina played with her hair suggestively and asked me some banal questions about my favourite sports or something equally unoriginal.

I got to work diagnosing the repair I was there for and Tina finally left me alone. She disappeared upstairs and left me to my work. It only took about 30 minutes or to so find the root-cause of the issue and repair it.

Just as I was wrapping up, Tina re-appeared, this

time, without the cropped jacket, and several top buttons open on her blouse, such that I could see her cleavage fully. What I hadn't noticed previously was just how large Tina's chest was. Without the jacket to constrain her breasts, her poor little blouse buttons were working overtime to keep everything in! I was wondering if it was just a small, tight fit, or if she purposely sized down to play up the size of her chest? Her blouse was so tight, and the strain such that I could could see through the openings between each button and into the "mysteries beyond", straight through to her tan skin beneath. Tina was not wearing a bra, and I could see the outline of her *very* erect nipples pressing against the fabric of her blouse!

Tina saw that I was looking and blushing…her obvious intention. She said to me in a sultry voice: "Don't worry, I like it when strong men look at me. It's what I was hoping you'd do. Do you like my tits?"

"…um…well, yes…they are lovely." I said with a gulp.

"It's ok - I want you to look at them. I want to show them off - they're new!"

"Oh, well in that case they're great! You must be very proud! Money well spent." I said awkwardly.

"Do you want to see them?"

I didn't know what to say. Obviously this was

inappropriate, and I felt that this situation was spiralling out of control very quickly. But before I could object or say anything to stop her Tina ripped open her shirt exposing her large, newly implanted, fully healed, beautiful, fake breasts.

"I got them for my husband, but he's never home, and he hasn't seen them yet. In fact they have not felt the touch of a man's hand yet," said Tina in a suddenly much more direct tone. "I want you to feel them"

With that—Tina snatched my hand and pushed it up against the side of her breast and moaned. She was *much* stronger than she looked!

"Mmm, I've waited so long for a big strong man to touch me like that."

"Oh. Well. They are fabulous!" I said as I started to sweat profusely.

A thousand horrible thoughts raced through my mind about what could happen because of this situation. Losing my job, losing my wife, being fined and put in jail for sexual harassment or worse—rape!. (It would be her word against mine and likely, I'd lose.)

"Use both your hands to grab my tits and then, kiss my neck." Tina commanded.

"I...uhh...I, can't." I stammered. "They are lovely breasts, and your husband is a very lucky man. But I'm married, and this is an inappropriate situation to be happening at work. I'm very sorry but I'll need my hand back." I said sternly as I began, as quickly as I could, to pack my tools and things into their case.

I half-walked, half-jogged up the stairs toward their front entrance and the door beyond, as I dialled my manager on the phone, (I wanted to be sure I had a witness as to what might go down) saying:

"Your issue has been fixed, there will be no charge today, I'm sorry for the inconvenience."

Tina rushed after me, up the stairs like a cheetah chasing an ibex. I had no idea anyone could move that fast in high-heels!

"But you haven't given me everything *I needed* yet, please don't go!" Tina panted.

"I'm sorry, I have to go" was all I could muster as I closed the door behind me.

Thankfully, Tina didn't chase me outside. My manager asked me what the hell was going on and I told him as I threw my tools in my van, started it up, and roared out of her driveway and down the road. We had a good laugh about the whole thing. Thankfully my manager was actually understanding about the whole issue, made notes and told me that if anything were to happen (like an attempted lawsuit), that the company "had my back." I was a little leery, but it felt good to be re-assured at the time.

Nothing ever came of it. I, nor the company ever

heard from Tina again. Although, one day, years later —my wife and I actually ran into her working the register at a local grocery chain. Our eyes met and instantly she recognized who I was. Gone was the makeup, fancy clothes, and jewelry. Instead she was dressed plainly, and in comfortable, sensible shoes. She still had her implants, but she had an air of depression about her and I noticed no more wedding ring on her finger. I guess her husband divorced her. (probably for cheating!)

10

GURGLE GURGLE

I know I tell a lot of "sex" stories—but I find it just so strange that people do and say such private things with a stranger in their home. As mentioned previously—I don't judge, but I always wonder what's going through someone's mind when they decide to engage in such behaviour. This time was a little different; but not by not much.

I was called to this tiny inner-city home on a Tuesday. I don't know why I recall that specific detail, but it was, in fact, a Tuesday. I was there to repair internet service as apparently the WiFi had been cutting in and out and causing issues for this customer's home based business.

I strode up to the door and rang. I was greeted by a "goth" girl in full makeup and outfit. I mention this as it seemed a little strange given that it was a Tuesday at about 10am, and not a Saturday night. But to each their own I suspect. Elise, we'll call her, was also wearing a full length, black-lace gown. Again—not to beat a dead horse here, but it was a Tuesday morning! It was intricately detailed and looked lovely for a night out on the town sucking blood.

Elise waved me into the home and gave me a quick tour. It was a very tiny house. One hallway with a bedroom and bathroom off to the right and a living room off to the left with a kitchen beyond. That was it. Perfect for the young, up-and-coming, vampire-couple on the town!

The wiring and equipment had all been setup in the living-room, as was sometimes the practice with older homes with no basement. So I began testing to find the problem. Elise left me alone and retired to the bedroom, just opposite the hall from the living-room where I was working.

Within a few moments of her leaving the room I could hear some muffled voices and shuffling around coming from the bedroom. She was not alone! No big deal for me, as I wasn't here on a social call—I had work to do. I kept my head down and got to work determining what, (if anything), was the problem. As it turned out, as is so often the case, there was no issue with the equipment nor the connection. I could not find a single error or issue that could be the source of the problem. I determined that there must be some interference within the home causing the WiFi issues for her. I called out to her because further testing would be needed.

"Hey, Elise?" I called out. "Could you join me in the living room for a moment?"

"Gurgle, gurgle, slurp, Ok."

"Well that was odd." I muttered under my breath.

In another few moments, I was joined in the living-room by Elise—still in full vampire getup. I described that there was no issue to be found and there must be an item in the home causing interference with the WiFi. I asked which room the issue was happening in, and sure enough it was the bedroom.

Now would be a good time to mention that there was a large mirror on the wall smack between the WiFI router and the bedroom beyond. Such as you do —placing a mirror in the main hallway leading out of the house so you can check your appearance before leaving for the day. Well…that's the problem! I pointed to it and began to describe to Elise the issue with WiFi signals and mirrors. (They don't work well together). She asked me what could be done. I told her nothing, "unless you know how to change the laws of physics." At which point she scoffed and said:

"Well there must be something."

I then gave her three options. One: move the wifi router into the bedroom which would require reworking outside wiring and drilling more holes in the side of her home; two, moving the mirror (apparently not an option); and three, running a computer cable from the router to the bedroom so that the computer there could be hard-wired. She chose the last option. But not before she asked if I could give her a couple of minutes of privacy in her bedroom as she had to clean-up. I of course agreed. After she entered the bedroom again, more gurgling and slurping occurred. I knew what kind of "cleaning" she was doing in there. <wink wink>

A few minutes later, the door to the bedroom opened and Elise said I could enter to do the required work. As it turns out—I had been right. She had been performing fellatio in the bedroom! Craziest part though—the dude was still naked, on the bed in the middle of the room! He was strapped to the bed, and had a metal contraption locked around his privates, aside from that, nothing abnormal! Oh—and there were lights, a camera and various other bits of filming and sound equipment in the room as well.

Elise explained that she and her partner were amateur gothic-porn producers. They had been filming their latest episode of "Ejacula". Horrible naming aside—I congratulated them on their business and asked why they didn't just wait till I had left, or reschedule for another time. She mentioned that they had a production schedule to uphold and they needed to get this scene shot this morning so they could edit it and upload it later that day. I said I understood and told them I'd be as quick as I could. Naked guy thanked me as he said he was starting to get uncomfortable in the cage and straps.

I finished the cable run quickly, and plugged in their computer. All was well, I said. I was finished and asked if there was anything else I could do.

"You could join us for a threesome, while we film it, we'll pay you for your time."

I was totally taken off-guard. I was flattered but explained that I was not allowed to do "side work" while on the clock for the cable company. (Besides being married, I wasn't into

random three-ways, goth chicks, or other dudes—but I didn't want to be rude so I wasn't about to tell them that!) Elise handed me a business card and said if I ever re-considered, I should call her.

I never did.

Funny note: I later was watching some adult entertainment videos online, and guess who's videos showed up as a recommended watch? You guessed it —Elise and friends! HA! They had quite the collection of videos and seemed that they were very popu-lar! It also appeared that the fellow I met the day that I interrupted filming was not her "regular" filming partner.

No judgement.

11

THE BUCKET

My job was not particularly hard. Sure, I had to deal with unpleasant customers, the cold, the wind, the rain, the snow, weirdness, smells, urine, vomit, unwanted sexual advances, constant horrible traffic, know-it-alls, and hard-to-please people; but, for the most part—I really liked the day to day of my job. I *can* tell you however how badly I needed to pee most of the time. Working alone, and from a service vehicle you always have the chance to pull over and piss on the side of the road, or stop at a McD's or 7-eleven and use the washroom for a #2. Occasionally, however, you'd be stuck out in the sticks and this wasn't an option.

On this particular day—I was working out in the rural area and I had to take a big #2. Now—as far as I was ever aware there was no formal "no using customer bathrooms" rule—but it was kind of frowned upon and *most* customers wouldn't be pleased if you left a big "Cleveland Steamer" in their toilet. (Flushed or not). I held it for as long as I could. I was really proud of myself—I actually made it through the job and out the door before the panic really set it. Once I returned to my truck though, I knew I was in trouble. "A turtle head" does not even begin to describe what was happening. I floored the truck to try and make it as far from the house as possible. I made it to the end of the concession road and turned the corner. I pulled the truck over and frantically ran to the back of the truck thinking I could just use the ditch or something... but that day for whatever reason—there was more traffic on the road than I had ever seen before. I was going to have to relieve myself in the back of my work van!

I grabbed one of the empty cable boxes and pulled the plastic liner bag out of it. Then I grabbed an old bucket that I kept in my truck for spare parts, and I dumped it on the floor of the van. I put the plastic bag in the bucket, pulled my pants down, sat on the bucket and exploded. It was a great relief! It smelled something awful though. The Indian curry I had had the night before mixed with the coffee and McMuffin™ I'd grabbed for breakfast did not mix well while they were in my guts. To say it smelled rotten would be generous at best.

After the explosion of foulness subsided, I realized that I had nothing to wipe with! I had some industrial hand wipes, (coated with pumice and lemon degreaser), some pieces of cardboard, and my undershirt. Well—degreasing hand wipes it was. Followed by my undershirt because I couldn't walk around for the rest of the day with pumice in my anus! I cleaned everything up, sealed the bag in the bucket and put the lid on the bucket. Then, promptly forgot about it!

It wasn't until two or three days later that I was cleaning out my truck back at the dispatch compound that I found the bucket. I pulled it out of my truck. Thankfully the bag and the lid had kept the smell contained—but after 2 days baking in the back of my van in the middle of summer—I can only imagine the unholy odour that would have come from it had the lid been opened! I decided not to take the lid off and I threw it into the dumpster behind the compound after wrapping some electrical tape around the lid. I then promptly forgot about it again.

That is until 3 weeks later, during our team meeting when someone brought up the bucket of shit they found in the dumpster. Now, I never did find out why they were dumpster diving in the first place, nor did I find out why they were opening buckets with tape around their lids. But I *do* know that they did both of those things. Apparently they also were so frantic in opening the lid to the bucket that they actually catapulted the contents of the bucket several yards across the parking lot and it hit the side of their work van! HA! We called him stinky from then on!

Oddly—nobody ever found out that it was my bucket! (Well, until now that is.)

12

SURPRISE BROADCAST

I always get a kick out of seeing funny, strange, unique, and interesting art, books, movies, and "stuff" in people's homes. It's an easy jumping-off point to ask questions and put people at ease—allowing them to talk about themselves. I remember one time a client had a massive collection of World War II medals, badges and other memorabilia. Another client, in a *very* well-to-do section of town, had an exotic car collection. Most people simply have knick-knacks or lots of movies. This fellow collected movies.

This particular day I was in a nice, newer neighbourhood, in a nice newer house, with a nice, newer family. Seriously—mom and dad with a new baby, probably weeks-months old. They also had *his* parents living with them in the house. It was a multigenerational home, not uncommon these days, but a little less common in this particular section of town. No matter, really; it doesn't affect the story, it just made things a bit more awkward, but more on that in a bit.

This particular call was an issue with "WiFi". However, what the call centre and dispatch had failed to ask was if whether the problem was on *our* devices or customer owned equipment. On this particular day, the problem was in fact with the customer's own equipment and had nothing to do with the internet service provided to the home. No matter—I was on site, and the customer was expecting me to fix his stuff—after all I was the face of the company and he had been promised that a technician would fix his stuff. So—google to the rescue!

I often joked with my co-workers that I would have my business cards changed to show E.C. Douglas, *"let me google that for you"*, because it was such an integral part of my job. Frankly I'll never understand how people can not do this for themselves and instead would prefer to waste time, and often money, to have a technician to their home to do the exact thing they could have done in the first place —for free! But…I digress.

The issue that the customer was having was: he

couldn't get his third-party streaming devices to stream properly to the TVs in the house. He had four. One in the master bedroom, one in the living room, one in the kitchen, and one in the parents' suite downstairs. They were all the same make and model, and all *should have* been compatible with his phone. However, every time he paired his phone to one of the devices it would display "paired" but nothing would stream from the phone to the television. Not exactly the desired behaviour for a streaming device.

We tested all the devices and they were all working independently. Such that if you turned it on with the supplied remote, the device would connect to the internet and the far end services and you could stream Netflix, Youtube, etc., etc. But the second he attempted to pair his phone—no go. I attempted my phone and it seemed to work ok on the devices. So I deduced that the issue must be with his phone. We tried a software update, an OS update and a few other bluetooth "fixes" I found on Google to no avail. Then I found a possible fix that might have just been the answer to our woes.

Apparently there was some sort of bluetooth interference issue for these streaming devices and his particular model of phone. So the work around fix was to turn off bluetooth on all the devices, and on his phone, then make sure all the devices were on the same WiFi network. Adding them one by one to a special "whole system remote" app that we found from the manufacturer's website. So we downloaded the app, made the adjustments in the settings for each device, then started discovering and adding each device to the smart phone app's dashboard.

The next step, the instructions told us, was to then try a simultaneous broadcast from the phone to all devices at once. Then to cycle through them one by one. Once that was complete—the system was setup and he would be able to choose the appropriate TV from the dashboard on the app, and stream whatever he wanted to it.

So that's exactly what he did. The only problem was, the file he chose to stream to *all TVs at the same time* was a porn movie. Apparently he was a collector of this stuff; I don't think he chose that file on purpose—it might have just been the last thing he had been watching—no matter, that's what was playing. Now, had it just been me, I wouldn't have cared; but, this fella's wife *and* elderly parents were all home at the same time. The movie suddenly sprang to life on all the screens at once in ultimate HD glory! Full sound FX and all! Also, for some unknown reason—all the TVs were cranked way up. To say this guy had *extreme* tastes in porn was an understatement. This was not your playful cute porn of the 70's or 80's, this was hardcore, dungeon, punishment type stuff…with lots of…well, you don't need all the gory details. Let's just say this was some seriously shocking stuff—especially for a family man.

The wife started screaming: "What is going on, shut it off, shut it off!"

His parents were silent and transfixed. I'm not sure they had ever seen or heard anything like the depraved actions occurring on their screen at the moment. The problem was, because it was streaming to all the TVs at once—there was a delay as he tried to cancel the broadcast—and so he ended up hitting so many buttons at once that the app froze! So the porn just kept hammering away on the screen.

Thinking fast—I darted around the house and manually shut off each TV to kill the offending images and sounds. He was still staring at his phone, in a kind of daze. The wife, now crying, came out from the master bedroom, new baby in her arms, asking "what in the world had he been watching?" He just stood there, dumbfounded, and offered no answer.

Thinking that I would try to save this guy's hide —I offered a lame excuse, and said that the video was mine. I apologized saying that I had selected it by mistake. But the wife didn't believe it. She politely asked if I would leave as it was clear the issue was fixed now, and she glared at the husband saying "We have a lot to talk about."

I excused myself to my van where I promptly broke out in laughter. I drove away thinking about that poor guy and the brow beating and guilt-tripping he would have to endure for who knows how long. But, "all in a day's work for me", I said out loud in my van for no particular reason. I had another call to get to and I didn't have time to ponder anymore on the awkward moment I had just been a part of; so with that, I carried on with my day.

13

THE HOARD

*I*f you've ever watched that show *Hoarders*, you know what this story is going to be about from the get go. But what they don't ever really talk about on that show is the smell. There are many different types of hoarders, and many different reasons for hoarding; however, one thing remains constant: once the piles get big enough, and the house gets full enough—food, animals, and other things end up getting forgotten about and piled on top of, and that forgotten biotic matter starts to rot.

That rotting matter, depending on what it is and how long it's been rotting, will have slightly different odours. Usually you can smell it walking up to the house. A "new" hoard will usually smell slightly acrid; but old, long established, long—sitting hoards will have layers of funk—kind of like a really old, ripe, cheese. The pile has sat for so long that it starts to develop different characteristics. And of course, if the people were smokers or not will add an even denser putrescence to the miasma. Then, of course, depending on the level and size of the hoard—bathrooms, kitchens, sinks may be clogged/filled with water and gone stagnant. And then of course, there is mould, mildew, and other fungus to contend with.

Suffice it to say, hoarding houses pose *significant* health and safety risks for anyone attempting entry.

On this particular day I was called to do a repair for a lady in her late 60's, and on the previous tech notes I saw: "house is extremely messy", which if someone has gone to the trouble to note, it's usually pretty bad. Well, that turned out to be the understatement of the year!

I could smell the hoard as soon as I walked through the gate and was within "nose shot" of the house—about 30 feet. Old, unwashed feet, mixed with rotten food, stale cigarette smoke, old, stagnant water, and something that I would later discover was several dead cats (in the back yard). The lady didn't answer her door; instead, she opened a window next to the door and told me I needed to come around to the back entrance, as it was easier to get into the house that way.

As I walked around back I saw the three dead cats strewn about the yard. Positioned with their heads facing away from the house, with paws outstretched as if they were trying to escape the disgusting nightmare that was inside. I guess, technically, they had indeed made it out.

I entered the house and was immediately greeted by about 3 dozen house flies, and the site of garbage, literal garbage, piled up to the ceiling in every room, with a little path cut through to get from room to room. The lady was having issues with her phone and said it didn't work. However, judging by the state of the yard and the back entrance, I knew that the issue was likely mold/mildew or other filth shorting out a jack somewhere in the house.

Thankfully, inside wire is the responsibility of the home owner, and I was able to verify services were working to the demarcation point on the outside of the house (the point at which legally the phone company's responsibility ends, and the home owner's responsibility begins). I was able to tell her that the phone service was working, and unfortunately the issue was inside her home, and I was not going to be able to get around in her house and access the jacks to determine which outlet was causing the issue. She didn't put up a fight, as if she knew why/what was going on. She thanked me for my time and I left. I reported the home to our safety department, and I believe that no tech is allowed to be booked back to that house unless it is cleaned, and they have a manager accompany them to the site for verification of safe work site.

I now have a rule for myself—if I can't walk through your door/hallway/rooms upright, carrying my tool bag as I would normally walk, then your home is a safety hazard, and I will declare it as such, and I will refuse service. Sadly, I've had to use this rule a total of 4 times in my 18 year career! Unbeliev-able but true!

14

THE OUTAGE

It's not uncommon to be called out to homes for internet/cable TV issues when there is a power outage. For some reason people think that the internet company can fix their power so their internet equipment and computers/phones, etc will work before the power company resumes normal service to their home. You would think that the call centre agents would scan for these things or at least ask—but sadly they do not, and it is an all-to-common issue that I get sent to "fix" the internet when the home has no power. On this particular day, I was called to a home in one of the oldest neighbour-hoods in the city for just such an occasion.

I rolled up to the house and all seemed normal. It was a nice 1.5 storey unit with a basement and all seemed perfectly normal. The phone, internet, and TV were not working. I didn't even think to ask about the power, as it was daytime and there was no need for lights. But as I got into the house I got a weird sense that something wasn't right. This wasn't a hoarder house, but I could tell there was a sense of loss/grief, or maybe just "crazy" floating through the air? It turns out that the lady of the house had just lost her husband and she was still very much in the process of grieving. So that answered that question!

I verified the services were working to the demarcation point outside the home (phone and internet signal was working) so I informed the customer that the issue was likely inside wire and I'd need to access the basement to find the short.

No sooner had she taken me over to the basement door than I suddenly understood what the issue was. I have no idea how it happened, or what could even cause this type of catastrophe—but her entire basement was flooded! Not with sewer backup, mind you, but what seemed like clean/fresh water. And the water was all the way up to the third step down to the basement. She had a swimming pool for a basement! The water was high enough that it had shorted out the power to the house and caused the main breaker to blow, thus protecting the house from a major fire incident. (Obviously our services weren't going to work either!)

She hadn't even noticed in her state of grief. Immediately, I got her out of the house, as I wasn't sure if the water was still running, if the power was live, or if any other dangers were present. I was able to call the power company and the fire department to make sure the power was off/disconnected to the home—it was then deemed safe for us to go back in the house to gather up a few of her things. Her only family was a son, and he did not live in the same city but was a few hours away. I made arrangements with him to come to town and I put the lady in a taxi to take her to a hotel, where she would stay for the next few days until they could figure out what to do but not before I helped her call her insurance company so they could send an assessor/claims adjuster to inspect the damage and get the repairs started. Plumbers, engineers, and a water damage company came to take care of the place.

At the end of it all I never did get any followup from the family, no thank you note, no recognition for my part in helping her with this, and of course no explanation of why/how this had happened. That's not why I helped, but it would have been nice to followup and make sure it all turned out ok, I think they must have sold the house/property, because I drove by about 6 months later and it was an empty lot with a new basement being poured, and from what I could see the account was no longer active in our systems.

15

WAIT—HOW MANY NAKED STRIPPERS WERE THERE?

*S*ome days it just doesn't pay to get out of bed and drag my ass to work. Other days you work in a place with a bevy of incredibly beautiful, naked, and VERY friendly strippers walking around.

That is all…next story.

Nah, I'm kidding - I couldn't do that to you. Here's the goods…

This house was like pretty much every other house on the block, although I did notice a few CCTV cameras on the corners of the home and at the car port, and there was a BIG black Mercedes van/people transporter with completely blacked out windows parked out front. Which I thought was odd —but likely another of the "tin foil hat" brigade (of which there seem to be many).

Upon knocking on the door—a rather dumpy upper-middle-aged skinny dude opened the door. You know the type: cigarette hanging out of his mouth, thinning hair brushed over too much scalp making the top of his head look like a bar code, a strange and perfectly round beer belly poking out between his shirt and his joggers. I figured for SURE this guy was some sort of security nut/conspiracy head. He asked me to present my ID badge, give him my card, show him my work order, and allow him to call my cell phone to verify who I was (as if the giant company-branded vehicle parked out front of his house, and all the ugly branded clothing I was wearing, wasn't enough proof?!)

Anyway—he let me into the house and he explained that he "had to be careful" because he ran "a sort of hostel" and there were many people that would try and break in to cause damage to his property, or harass his guests. (Great, I'm thinking, I've walked into some sort of drug haven.) As it turns out he tells me that this "hostel" is for out-of-town strippers who do feature dancing at the local strip clubs, and he runs a full service business for them—picks them up at the airport, shuttles them back and forth to the clubs, and, of course, provides a place for them to sleep, eat, train, tan, and relax while not on shift.

Hence my arrival to install internet and TV services. Only catch is, he says, is that all the girls are sleeping right now so I have to be quiet and I can't enter any of the bedrooms to do work for at least another couple hours. I tell him that's fine as I have a bunch of work to do outside first (to put in a new service line, upgrade grounding, electrical protection, etc., etc.) and it would likely take me about 1.5 hours outside before I was ready to come inside and do all of the individual TV hook ups. He thought that was great and said I could come and go out the back door as I needed.

So I got to work and after about 1.5 hours everything outside was upgraded and ready to go, and I was ready to now move into the house to do my inside work.

As I entered the back door—I happened to lock eyes with a stunning, nearly perfectly proportioned (except for her almost comically oversized breasts) blonde as she was sitting in a tiny little nightie at the kitchen table drinking coffee, and I don't mind saying that I could see all of her details under the "nightie" that might as well not even have been worn, for all the coverage it gave her. If her name was Victoria she sure didn't have any secrets left.

She offered to make me a cup of coffee and I gladly accepted as it had been quite chilly out that morning. Her cute little butt wiggling as she walked around the kitchen was very distracting.

I'm a happily married man, and I pride myself, especially at work, to not ogle women, but I could not help myself from stealing more than a few peeks while she bounced happily around the kitchen making my coffee. She brought it over to me in the next room as I was working down low on a TV jack; as she bent down to hand it to me her sweet perfume nearly knocked me out. It was all I could do to not fall over between that delicious scent and the fact that her very obviously enhanced breasts were dangling in my face. She must have sensed that I was a little embarrassed, because with a giggle she snapped back upright, flashing the briefest glance at her completely bare pubic area, then she turned to walk away as she gave her butt another little shake.

I think she must've woken up all the other girls in the house at that point because one by one, they began to appear, almost making it a point to parade past me either completely naked, or just wearing a g-string, or perhaps a skimpy top. The reason I say this is that it seemed like they were playing a game with me, almost as if they had bets going on as to which girl could make me blush or blunder or god knows what their end game was!

I had to install TV boxes in each bedroom—filled

with skimpy outfits, lacy underwear, toys, props, and heady scents. All the while I had to deal with teasing questions from the gorgeous young occupant of each room while trying to focus on just doing my job and not being an ogling pervert. I got through the individual rooms without incident. A couple of the rooms were multi-occupancy (I think 3 girls was the fullest one). I was in teenage boy fantasy land.

At one point in the main room, which had a big screen TV, two couches, and a pool table, there was me and I think 6 naked strippers all chatting with each other and talking to me—asking me questions about my job, about the TV service, and some other very personal questions about my married life, if I was happy, "what's the kinkiest sex I ever had with my wife", etc., etc. Some of them asked me to help them choose between two outfits. One asked which lipstick I liked better. One of them showed me a new "prop" that she had purchased for insertion. I have to tell you I have never looked *so intently* at my tools in my entire career as at that particular moment! I will admit that I stole quite a few glances because of the wondrous variety of looks and types of beautiful bodies that were before me! I had never seen so many beautiful women in one place at once! If I had been at the club where these girls worked I would have had to pay hundreds if not thousands of dollars to see them all this up close and personal. All in all I counted 15 beautiful ladies that day.

It all came to a head when, as I was finishing up the installation and I was handing my business card to the homeowner; two of the girls started passionately making out behind him caressing each other—I could barely stand it anymore—I hoarsely said my final words and blurted something out like, "it's been an enjoyable morning spending time with all of you lovely ladies, take care of yourselves and I'll remember you all fondly," or something equally awkward, cringeworthy and lame.

As I was walking away, Mr. Dumpy followed me out to my truck and said something menacing like "now you forget where I live and don't ever tell anyone where we are or there'll be consequences." To which I said "no problem man." I got in my truck and high-tailed it out of there to go find myself a cold beverage and think about anything other than sparkly boobies and clean shaven privates. That evening the wife and I certainly had some very extra specially heated love making. I told her all about it of course and she said she didn't care where I got my appetite, as long as I came home for dinner!

16

THE COUGAR

The region that I live and work in is varied when it comes to terrain. Although most of my work is "city" some of my jobs take me to the outskirts, which technically we call the "fringe" but in reality is "rural" or if you're feeling salty "the sticks". On this particular late winter/early spring day I was sent out to the fringe to deal with a no dial tone issue on a home phone. The property was a good 40 minute drive out of the city and was in a nicely wooded/hilly area outside of town. Beautiful, I love it, I wouldn't like to live out there—but it's amazing to look at and nature is right in the back yards of the homes there.

I pull up to the house, and it's a grand affair designed in a very modern style. Lots of squared corners, tall and grey, windows that are long and rectangular that run the length of the exterior walls. It was a sight to behold—and the landscaping didn't disappoint either! The driveway, yard and property was outlined and defined by massive grey flagstones built into a multi-stepped wall almost resembling the stepped pyramids of South America. As I looked around the back of the house, I could see that the property and house were built into the back of a hill such that the back yard had to have been excavated out of the hill, and the giant flagstones were in place as a sort of stepped retaining wall to keep the trees and dirt/hill in place. They had an outdoor fire pit, what I can only assume was a 30 or 40 person hot tub jacuzzi, and a fully tiled outdoor bbq area with seating, lights, and a trellis for climbing vines that at the current time were hibernating because of the cold. I scouted out the property; the point of demarcation (where my testing begins) was in the back yard.

So I circled the property fully and went to the front door to ring the bell. I didn't even have to knock before a young man, dressed in formal attire answered the door. I introduced myself and explained why I was there, and he mentioned that the lady of the house had been expecting me, and if I could please do my work quickly as they needed their phone for a family emergency that was currently occurring. I said I would do my best and walked around to the back of the home to start my testing.

I opened the box containing the connections that I needed to examine, and as I was squat down doing my work, I felt like I was being watched. I looked around and I didn't see anyone, so I continued about my business, coming and going over the next 30 minutes or so, as I tested their phone lines and determined what the problem was. Each time I returned to the back of the house I had the same eerie feeling like I was being watched, but I couldn't see anyone around so I thought it was just the effect of the massive home and the secluded location making me feel paranoid.

But during my last visit to the connector box, I finally saw who had been watching me.

I looked back behind me and there, at the top of the stepped flagstone wall, was a massive cougar. It must have been 150 pounds if it was an ounce. It sat quietly observing me, not moving, as if to say "I approve of your presence, but I will supervise your work."

It was so large and so close it literally took my breath away. I've done enough reading about predatory animals to know that you don't run from them, as that will trigger their hunting instincts and they will chase you—the last thing that I wanted that day was to fight for my life against 150 pounds of pure, deadly muscle and razor sharp "technician-killing claws". So I merely continued my work as I had been, and then slowly stood up, very calmly, and said "Well, I'm all done here" then walked slowly back around to the front of the house.

I rang the door again; this time another young man in formal clothes answered the door. I advised them that the problem had been fixed and he checked the cordless phone by the entrance, and we made a couple of quick test calls in and out with my cell-phone to confirm, and all was right again. He thanked me for my time and handed me a crisp $100 bill as a tip. I thanked him as I shook his hand and folded the bill into my pocket. I also asked him briefly if the family knew about the cougar out back that "overlooked" their property. He said that they suspected that "something was back there, as the owners' prized dogs keep disappearing," then continued on to tell me that they had never actually seen or captured the culprit! I informed him of what I saw and advised he call the local animal control/parks officers to report the sighting.

With that, I headed back to my van, got in, and drove away, thanking my lucky stars that I was going home safe that day!

17
______

THE "REST" HOME

*S*ometimes when working, life surprises you. People surprise you. What am I talking about? *Sometimes*...Ha! Let me rephrase that...

Everyday I am surprised by people. Sometimes it's because of a thing they say, sometimes it's the things they do, sometimes it's the situations that happen while I'm in a home.

This particular experience was kind of a combination of all of those things.

I had been called to an assisted living seniors care facility for a "no dial tone" issue for what I assumed, based on the name, was an elderly lady. These types of calls are fairly typical in these places since residents are sometimes moved from room to room because of deaths, changes in level of care, or some-times just fora change of scenery. Either way—often the staff simply moves the resident from room to room, assuming that the phone line will "magically" migrate with the resident, even though no one bothers to call the phone company to do a move. More often than not the resident moves rooms, attempts to make a phone call out, and they have no dial tone. It's an easy fix that requires about 10 minutes worth of re-wiring for the customer in the main telephone room of the care facility. (Usually a dark musty room in the basement) But all in all, a simple fix, and I'm generally glad to do them as they provide for a breather in the middle of otherwise completely hectic days.

This care home was a posh affair, with fresh cut flowers in the lobby, a live pianist playing a baby grand in the reception area and a grand fountain in the courtyard. I was impressed—I had never been in such a lavish facility before! I took a glance around, smiled at the piano player and made my way to reception, where it is customary to sign in and provide ID and a work order number to get a "site pass" that allows onsite staff to know that you are authorized to be there. I did this without incident and was instructed on how to get to the resident's room and told that she should be there awaiting my arrival.

I went upstairs, followed my instructions to turn left out of the elevator and proceeded down the hall to the last door on the left before the emergency exit stairs. I knocked on the door and there was no answer. (Not unusual.) So I waited for a few moments, expecting that the old lady would likely need a few moments to get up out of her chair and get over to the door.

After about 5 minutes there had still been no answer, so I knocked again, and again—waited.

10 minutes or so passed without answer so I made my way back to the nurses station on that floor to let them know and was told "no, she's in there, just knock and go ahead on in." Which again is "normal", in that sometimes patients are old/sleepy/bed ridden and sometimes can't get up to answer the door. She must have been sleeping, I thought to myself as I walked back down the hall toward the room.

I once again stood in front of the door—crocheted, pastel crucifix in the middle of the door staring me in the face—knocked and went in.

Inside the door was a dimly lit hallway that led to the bathroom on the right and a main living room area beyond, with, I'm assuming, the bedroom off to the left. I announced myself and said I was there from the phone company to fix their phone issue, with no response at all. I walked a little further into the hall and entered the living room. It was at this point that I could hear what sounded like struggling and heavy breathing coming from the bedroom. My senses perked up and the adrenaline started flowing as I assumed the poor old girl was having a seizure, stroke, or heart attack. So I again announced who I was and pushed the door open to a scene that will live in my memory forever.

There on a hydraulically lowered hospital bed was the old woman naked on all fours flanked on either side by two older men, one at each end of her!!! She was making gurgling noises from her throat since her mouth was filled by the one fella and her other end was being attended to by the second man's raging viagra induced passion. And both men had their hands held high in a double "high five" position, leaning on each other for support in what I later learned is called the "Eiffel tower."

I noticed all of this in a split second as the man at the rear end of her looked at me and snapped, saying, "There was a reason we didn't answer the door; now either get naked and help us gang bang this old slut, or get the fuck out!"

I was a little blushed in the face to be sure!

I attempted an apology as I backed out of the room quickly, closing the door behind me, and stumbling over a table or footstool on my way back through the living-room. I made a beeline for the suite door and then closed it tightly behind me. Quickly, calmly, I moved back to the nurse's station where the nurse asked me if I was able to "service the resident's needs?" It was all I could do to not laugh out loud. I told them that she was indisposed at the moment and requested a reschedule; I left a standard business card and let them know they could call us at anytime.

I made it all the way to my van, but had not put my tools away before I couldn't hold it in any longer. I lost it completely and laughed so hard I cried. It was a fantastically funny situation and looking back wasn't too bad. The old woman had been in remarkably good shape, and despite their saggy balls and big-old beer bellies, the old men seemed to be virile as well. (Even if medically induced.)

It's given me hope that even at an old age I'll still have the want and need for intimacy, or at the very least pure lustful enjoyment of other naked people! Apparently old-folks' homes are hotbeds of this kind of fornication on a regular basis. Also accompanied by a rise in the STD rate amongst senior citizens—but

I suppose since they are so close to the end they don't really care anyway—makes sense: enjoy life while you can!

Vivre centenaire!

18

EVICTED

*U*sually when I go to apartment buildings or townhouse complexes to do installs— it is at the rental units in the complex because most of the people that live in these complexes own their units, but more and more are being turned into rental units seemingly on a weekly basis.

So there was was nothing unusual about being called to this particular complex in the city's north side to do an install. I called ahead and left a voice mail, which is usual these days as most people don't answer their phones anymore, especially for numbers they don't recognize.

So I arrived on site to the complex, a boring beige series of buildings slightly more attractive than subsidized housing, but not by much. There were no flowers in the pots outside, no attractive window coverings—just plain, beige stucco with white trim. Yuck.

The only nice thing about this complex was that there was clearly demarcated guest parking, surprisingly right next to the main entrance of the building that I needed to attend to.

I rang the buzzer for the unit I was to be installing and again I got voice mail. At this point it was not looking good to be able to complete this install because there was no contact with the customer, and I wasn't getting into the secure building. (Despite what people think I don't have a master/skeleton key for all buildings in the city!)

Anyway, just as I was getting ready to call my dispatcher to log the job as incomplete, a young couple, frantically waving their arms, approached my van. They explained that they were Dan and Alicia and were the tenants that I was there for; however, there was a problem.

Apparently the last tenant refused to leave the apartment and they were working on getting access and possession of the unit from the manager. It was at this point that suddenly 3 police cruisers showed up at the building, sirens and lights blazing, and 6 police officers got out of the cars and all casually walked up to the door of the building, after turning off their sirens, but leaving their engines running and lights spinning.

They were there to forcefully remove the aforementioned tenant! I learned later that the tenant had lapsed rent and been evicted some 4 months previously but the landlord couldn't get him to leave, and after serving several court orders and other measures, finally he resorted to calling the police to execute the eviction that day! So while the new tenants and I were standing and waiting outside, the Police entered the premise, and about 10 minutes later left escorting a very skinny, very dirty young man from the building and into the back of one of the police cars, where presumably they were reading him his rights and processing paperwork to take him to jail, or wherever they were taking him…

It was an extremely awkward event; nobody seemed to know what to do. The young man's family came to clear out his stuff from the apartment; as the landlord was frantically trying to clean, the new tenants were trying to move some stuff in, and I was trying to install their internet! HA! The family of the previous tenant kept shooting us dirty looks the entire time—and finally the new tenant looked at who I assume was the young man's mother and said

"Well if he had paid his rent or simply moved out like he was supposed to this wouldn't be happening."

Yuuuup.

19

I'M UP A POLE...I'LL WAIT

It wasn't "one of those days." It wasn't a dark and gloomy day. It was just a day like any other. It was winter, and chilly but not frigid, with a fresh powder coat of snow on the ground. I was working in the bad section of town. Most refer to it as "the hood" and I would fully agree. There is something somehow more real about poor neighbourhoods. People, while often distrustful of outsiders, usually have a pretty good relationship with many of their neighbours and will often look out for each other, all the while generally embracing their lot in life, and working hard and making do with what little they have.

I was called to do a "new" installation in a quadplex. When I use quotes around new I mean it was a brand new service install; the home, lines, alley, and poles out back were anything but new. On this particular street, time had performed it's inevitable dance and things were well worn down and clearly past their prime. Although the freshly fallen snow gave a nice camouflage coating to everything and made everything look just a little nicer! The houses and multi-tenant units were all built post world war two, so had that distinctive box shape and unremarkable architecture that allowed for rapid build times and quick possession. At one point, when this neighbourhood was new, it would have been a lovely place to live with picket fencing, cute gardens, and little garages out back just big enough for a single car. However, the current state belied the area's humble but respectable beginnings. Broken glass, used tires, drug paraphernalia strewn about, and lots of rotten food and other refuse tossed into the alley, all made my job just a little extra dangerous while moving out back to the pole to climb and hook up services.

I had my van parked near the pole, but not completely blocking the alley, safety cones out indicating that work was going on, and 4 way flashers with beacon on and rotating. I donned my climbing gear: safety glasses, hi vis vest, gloves, tool pouch, helmet, safety straps/harness, and spurs. I grabbed the pole, strapped in and began my assent. All went smoothly with no issues climbing up; I settled in and began working to make the necessary connections to get the customer in service.

Shortly after I was up and working, I heard some noise—some scuffling and raised voices—although I couldn't make out what was being said. I looked down and there were 2 people running down the street and up the alley I was working in. Actually, it looked like one man was chasing the other; yes, black coat was chasing blue coat. Neither were wearing hats or scarves, but it was clear that in the heat of the moment they didn't really need them. Quite quickly the man in black caught up to the man in blue and they struggled for a moment. More yelling in what I can only assume was Somali (again judging by the neighbourhood and the location of the mini-mall where I believe they had come from, where there were several Somali stores, a hair salon and a mini-mart). Then they seemed to embrace; however, when they let go of each other the man in black turned and ran quickly away, while the man in the blue coat stood for a moment as if in a trance, and then fell over.

The man in blue lay on his side not really moving, but groaning a little seeming to clutch his abdomen. I noticed a pool of bright red blood on the freshly fallen snow, and the stain was growing. He had been stabbed! I called 911 immediately using my cellphone and bluetooth headset.

"Hello, 911 what is your Emergency?"

"Yes, I'm a telecom worker and I'm in the alley behind 733 Lux Street, working up a utility pole and I have just seen a man get stabbed in the gut with a knife."

"Is the man alive and breathing?"

"I think so, but he's bleeding out quite quickly—you need to send the Police and an Ambulance right away."

"Are you alright? Where are you?"

"I'm up a pole right now. I'm safe. The man who stabbed him ran away."

"Can you wait until the Police show up to give a statement?"

"Yes, I can wait. Hurry!"

The Police showed up within 2 minutes and the EMS about 15 seconds after that.

They asked me to come down and give a statement once they had secured the area, while the EMS tended to the man's wounds and put him in the ambulance for transport to the hospital.

I told them what I could, time, location, details of direction they had run from and where the man in black ran to. I also mentioned that it seemed like they were speaking a foreign language but I couldn't be sure what, although most likely Somali.

They thanked me for my time and for calling 911, also telling me that I had likely saved the man's life.

I called my manager immediately after the events occurred and he asked me if I was alright. I mentioned that I was pretty shaken from the events, and the rush of adrenaline. I asked if I could go home for the rest of the day and he denied my request. He told me to "man up, stop being a pussy, and finish your work." No rest or reward for the cable guy I guess!

I never did hear from the Police again, or the man whose life I saved. And I never did get any consideration or counselling for the trauma that I witnessed. I guess all in all it wasn't really that traumatic. But still I think I should have at least been able to go home and have the rest of the afternoon off! That manager wouldn't even allow an extended break because the dip in productivity would negatively affect his numbers for the day/month. So I just had to suck it up.

It's management decisions like that, lack of respect and being treated like a number—that ultimately piled on top of each other and forced me to finally quit the business. That manager, by the way, is now some top director or operations manager, likely on his way to executive status, I'm sure. Sad really. No heart, no soul, no consideration for other humans. Just numbers and a psychopathic pursuit of power.

Yeah, I'm glad I quit.

20

NO INSURANCE

Sometimes you don't need a big pre-amble. "Just the facts", as they say.

The *very first week,* after I had completed my apprenticeship and had just received my own truck —I was parked and working up a pole, in an alley, working in a terminal. Across the alley from my truck, which had lights flashing, cones out on the ground, and me up a pole—was a garage. The garage opened and out backed a car. SMACK into the broad side of my work van! I couldn't believe it! I rushed down the pole to talk to the driver. He was an elderly Asian man, who didn't speak much English. But he had a wad of cash that he kept trying to put in my hand and he was repeating "no insurance, no insurance."

Sadly—corporate vehicle = corporate policy.

Everything has to be done by the book with a Police report and report to management, insurance, etc. Thankfully he had insurance, which covered the accident. But later we found out that he didn't want to put a claim through his insurance because I guess he had had enough accidents that if he had another one, he would have been deemed "uninsurable." I'm sure it was sad and stressful for him. Kicker is—there had been enough room in the alley to drive a garbage truck between my van and his garage! I know this because shortly after he left—that's *exactly what happened!* So perhaps it was for the best that he lost his driving privileges!

21

AT LEAST THEY AREN'T HUMAN!

Not every day in the trenches of cable guy land do you run into something gross, disturbing, weird, smelly, dirty, awful, etc. However, I would say at least every other day it happens! This is a story from one of *those* days. To be honest though: "I showed up, stayed clean, everyone was nice, and job was easy" doesn't really make for interesting reading, does it? The whole reason you are reading this book is FOR the dirty, gory details, right?

Sometimes people surprise you. Sometimes the most well put-together, well-dressed, intelligent-looking people are the most uneducated, rude, condescending idiots you could ever have the misfortune of meeting. Then, others could look or sound funny, seem stupid, be dressed poorly or for whatever reason give the impression that they are stupid, but through conversation you find that they are just the opposite from your impression. This was not one of those customers. To be fair to Frank he was not gross, he didn't smell, he wasn't a hoarder, and he was dressed well enough, but something was just slightly off with him. Hard to put a finger on exactly what it was—no lisp or deformity, no wandering eye or personal-space invasion; his manner was just *off*. He wouldn't make consistent eye contact, darting his eyes away from you after about 2 seconds, looking at something on the floor or ceiling, to then come back to make eye contact again for no more than 2 seconds, and do it all over again. It was a strange affectation, but still, not the worst personality that I've ever dealt with.

To be truthful I don't even remember why I was at Frank's house. I'm sure it was to repair something but it hardly matters for the purposes of this story. Let's just say I had to replace a piece of broken equipment.

Frank's house was a small humble bungalow, in an older section of town. Not "the hood" but not a new, beautiful, gentrified area; just a regular neighbourhood in an otherwise unremarkable section of the city. I distinctly remember his bright red fake shutters on the windows. The shutters themselves weren't ugly or of poor quality. It was just their installation was a bit off. I'm sure you've seen the type that don't open or close, but just sit on either side of the window for decorative purposes—know the kind I mean? Bright red, and clearly made of vinyl or some other plastic. From the road they looked normal, but as you approached the house you could see that these shutters were merely tacked on to the siding of the house, and there was a 1/2" gap between them and the windows—you'd think that if you're going to put up stupid fake shutters, at least you'd mount them so they appeared to be a part of the window, no? I guess not. No matter.

From the moment Frank opened the door and we introduced ourselves, I could feel that this would be "a weird one"—again, there wasn't anything particularly wrong with Frank (aside from the eye contact issue)…it was just, a feeling. When you deal with the public on a daily basis, in their own homes, you get a sense for this kind of thing, and my "spidey sense" was tingling.

I entered Frank's house and got to work inspecting and diagnosing his issues. As part of my checklist I always made it a point to turn on every TV in the house connected for service so that I could ensure the entire system was working properly.

Thankfully every room seemed cool. Not dirty, not super clean, but no strange sex apparatuses, no people in cages, no dead bodies. But, just when I thought I was in the clear - I opened the door to the last room in the house and JACKPOT!

Hundreds of skulls lining the walls, the floor, the ceiling, shelving, everything in this room was covered in skulls. I don't mean wallpaper or decorative/figurative things. I mean actual, honest to goodness, real skulls.

Just as I was taking this in, Frank came up behind me, talking in a very low voice at almost whisper volume.

"Don't be afraid, they are just cat skulls."

"Oh—that's good." I replied rather tentatively.

"At least they aren't human skulls" said Frank, almost proudly.

I wanted to ask what that meant, but before I could get that out of my mouth he continued:

"You see, I really love cats, but I'm allergic. So I started trying to stuff cats. I hoped that if I could clean their fur then I wouldn't be allergic anymore. But even after they are dead I'm still allergic. So I thought that if I couldn't have a cat because of the fur, I could maybe at least keep the cat skeleton around…but that freaked out my friends and family. So, I just started collecting cat skulls. From old barns, friends, neighbours, family —anytime anyone finds a dead cat they give it to me and I properly dispose of the body but keep the skull. I treat them with a special varnish and sealant so they will last a long time. This way I can have as many cats as I want—but my allergies don't go off!"

He said all of this with a smile and a look in his eyes as if he were a cat bringing me a dead mouse. It was pretty weird. I stuttered something like "that's cool man" and continued with my work as quickly as possible. I wrapped up without incident and cleaned up my tools and left over packaging from the new box I had installed for him.

As I was leaving his house Frank asked me if I would like to take a cat skull with me. I briefly thought about it, thinking for just a moment that I could maybe take it home and paint it, or carve it and make a piece of art with it. Then I thought better of it —I politely declined.

I left the house and went back to my truck, started it up, and drove around the corner to sit and do my paperwork for the job so that I was out of sight of the "cat-head house".

Funnily enough, a co-worker went to this same house a few months, or maybe years, later and had a very similar experience. We laughed about it together and we both agreed he was one of the weirder customers we had ever run into.

Odder still—my co-worker TOOK a cat skull as a tip! He actually mounted it on the dashboard in his work van! HA!

22

YES! YOU HAVE SOME!

*S*ome days—you just meet strange people. Some days you meet totally cool people.

Some days, you meet seemingly cool people that turn out to be creeps. Sometimes you meet people that have something to hide—and then other times, people are totally upfront and honest about themselves, their lives, and even things that *should* be secrets!

On this particular day I was working in an older neighbourhood just off downtown; I'll never forget— it was a cool fall day. One of those days where there is still just enough sunlight and daylight hours to create a warm glow and maybe even a little sunburn on your face, but the air is chilly and the leaves are starting to turn.

I pulled up to the old Victorian style, 3 storey

house at the end of a cul de sac and parked out front. I had tried calling the site contact several times before I made my way to the home but hadn't been able to connect with anyone. This isn't uncommon—I usually would try once, then again a few minutes later, and leave a message that I would be on my way. Then I would either get to the premise, and someone would be there, or I'd get a frantic phone call saying something to the effect of "Oh no! I totally forgot you were coming!" This particular day—no phone call, just a grinning balding man with round John Lennon style glasses greeting me at the door.

The installation was quite straight forward with no major kinks or issues that I could anticipate, and the fellow, I'll call him "Evgeny", showed me around and then said "Please do work, I'll be upstairs in office if you need me." (I will always remember his piercing blue eyes and thick Russian accent.) With that he turned his back and climbed the stairs to presumably return to work. So with that I set about getting his internet and tv hooked up.

The outside portion of work took me no more than about 15 minutes—to change and update some circuit protection and ensure the grounding was good. And inside, as mentioned, was quite straight forward, with cabling already running in the house from his electrical panel to all the TVs and rooms that required internet connection. All in all—I think I was in the home for about 2.5 hours.

I had finished up and packed all my garbage out to my truck, along with my tools and check lists. I came back in, expecting that Evgeny had heard me go in and out of the house and had probably seen me go out to my truck. But upon entering the house again—nobody was to be seen. I called out…silence. So I made the trek up the 3 flights of stairs to the upstairs office where Evgeny had said he would be. The door, of course, was closed. I knocked. No answer.

I knocked again…no answer. Strange I thought to myself…just to leave your home with a stranger in it? Suddenly the door opened.

"Yes?"

I was very surprised since I hadn't heard him get up or cross the room to open the door.

"I'm all set and finished; everything went very smooth—would you like me to give you a lesson on how to use the system?" I asked.

"No, but you come into office, I have for you special treat."

Thinking I was going to get another stale cookie and a copy of the watch tower, or perhaps an actual tip—I began to explain how tips weren't necessary… But before I could get a word out of my mouth—

Evegeny reached out a thick, hairy, arm. It was far more heavily muscled than I had noticed previously. He grabbed me by the shirt and pulled me into the room.

It must have been a sound proofed room as I had not heard any voices, and as it turned out there were 3 other *very large, very Russian* men in the room with him. All of them were drinking vodka and watching some sort of Eastern European music videos on a large screen projector image beamed onto the wall, with the sound off. Just then I noticed a large pile of what I thought was flour on the table in the middle of the room, and next to the giant pile was a digital scale and a box of baggies.

Well, I must have looked as white as a sheet because Evgeny said, "No problem, you have Vodka and relax. I want to give you special treat as thank you for service."

I stammered a little but he thrust the Vodka into my hand and I reluctantly drank it.

Then he says: "Is Cocaine. Yes! You have some!" Again, I tried to refuse. I have never done cocaine in my life, and come to think of it, up until that point I had never even seen it!

Evgeny and his buddies all started to laugh as one of them pulled out a mirror and razor blade and prepared two lines of cocaine, presumably for my consumption. The sweat was rolling down my forehead now. I really didn't want to be there, I really didn't want to try cocaine, and I especially didn't want to try cocaine with the Russian mob!

"We are Russian mafia," Evgeny boasted, "you will have cocaine, and you will never tell anyone about why we are here, or we kill you."

At which point I again protested and said something like "But I didn't even know about this—you could have just let me leave." Evgeny just laughed. They all laughed. One of them pulled out a gun and pointed it at me and said "You have some."

So…I bent down, and like I had heard about, read about, and seen in so many movies stuck a rolled up $100 bill into my right nostril and the other end to the line of powder and snorted it up. I switched nostrils and snorted the other line into the left nostril. Apparently this made the Russians happy, and they all clapped and laughed and said: "Now you are man", or something to that effect.

For those of you who have never done cocaine— it's hard to describe the rush that you feel suddenly all over your body. All I can tell you is I suddenly felt incredible, like I could take on the world and win! HA!

Evgeny—leaned toward me, folded a crisp $100

bill into my top pocket and said "Now you are one of us, yes?"

I nodded, and although I *felt* invincible I somehow knew that I wasn't, thankfully. With that—Evgeny slapped me on the shoulder and said: "Ok, enough! Now you go.".

I just nodded and turned and walked away with them cackling behind me.

Up until now—I have never told this story. Why would I? I was threatened by the Russian mafia, they gave me cocaine, booze, and money! I would lose my job for sure…not to mention maybe my life! We've all hear the stories—I wasn't about to attempt anything so severe as snitching! To this day, though, I still wonder why they did that. I suspect it was just some cruel joke, prank or their way to "have little fun with cable man." Either way—it was terrifying and electrifying all at the same time! I had never done anything like that before, or since.

First and last time. Now that is a real story from the crazy life of a cable guy!

ACKNOWLEDGMENTS

Firstly, I want to thank my wife for encouraging me to write this—and for staying out of my way and letting me do it. She's a much better writer than I, and very easily could have pushed herself onto me to edit, co-write, or re-write. She just let me do it, quietly believing in me and encouraging me. It doesn't seem like too much—but this volume took me nearly a year to complete. I think in total time it would look more like 3-ish months, start to finish, but with work and life happening—it was indeed the better part of a year.

So formally - thanks darling, I love you!

Secondly, I want to thank you, dear reader, again, for purchasing this book! I had a *lot of* fun remembering these stories. If this book does well—there is another volume that I would like to write. Why didn't I include those stories in this first book? "Gotta leave them wanting more" is the old theatre motto. I figured it applied here too.

I also want to thank all the co-workers that I've had over the years that gave me hope, encouragement, friendship, and guidance. Even though I no longer work with them—I think of them all fondly, and damn near daily something comes up that reminds me of one of them and it makes me laugh, smile, or even get a little choked up!

Lastly—to the men and women of the craft still working long, hard, thankless hours, getting dirty, and putting up with way more shit than they paid us for: thank you. Thank you for all you do to keep the country and world connected, entertained, and in this crazy time (I am currently finishing this book during the 1st COVID-19 quarantine) safe. I know what it's like—so know that if any of you ever come to my home in the future: I won't be naked, I won't be weird. I'll be friendly, kind, offer you a fresh drink from a clean glass; I will tip you, and I won't take no for an answer!

See you down the road!

E.C. Douglas